Praise for Make Money on Medium

"*Make Money on Medium* is for anyone who has always wanted to earn money as a writer but didn't know where or how to start. This comprehensive, step-by-step guide is all you need to get started. Nicole Akers opens up her storehouse of knowledge and shares a wealth of timely, actionable information with any writer who wants to take their writing to new heights."

-Jeff Goins, bestselling author of *Real Artists Don't Starve*

"As a full-time blogger and author, yet Medium newbie, I found Nicole Akers' incredible guide to be so encouraging, motivating, and jammed full with must-read insight. This book is your one-stop shop for how to engage and reach your audience online."

- Paul Angone, author of *101 Questions You Need to Ask in Your Twenties* and creator of AllGroanUp.com

"Nicole first caught my eye in early 2018. Her publication, **Publishous** had about 1,000 followers if I'm not mistaken. Here we are in mid-2019 and her publication has 19,800 followers now. The knack she has for attracting the best writers on Medium to contribute is incredible, and I love contributing at least 1 story per week because I always get great reach with **Publishous**. High view counts are a testament to how much her audience loves her publication. "*Make Money on Medium*" is a no-brainer if you want to learn pretty much everything there is to know about Medium from a seasoned veteran."

–Tom Kuegler, top writer on Medium.com

"*Make Money on Medium* is the perfect resource for any writer looking to get readers on Medium, as well as earn enormous income from their work. A must-read for any writer on Medium."

-Anthony Moore, top writer on Medium.com

"I've been the top-earning writer on Medium on 3 different occasions. I owe a large portion of my success to Nicole and her publication [Publishous]. Put one hundred percent of your trust in her because she knows exactly what she's talking about. Coming from a top writer, I can tell you the process she lays out is pretty much my entire recipe for making 4-5 figures a month on Medium every single month."

– Ayodeji Awosika, top writer on Medium.com and author of *You 2.0.*

"Nicole Akers is a fireball of energy and exuberance. But she's also a passionately committed writer, parent, and business person. And she has come to know Medium, inside and out, especially having established and grown her Medium publication, Publishous, to one of the Top 400 on the site within a year. You should pay attention and listen to her. I do."

– Caroline DePalatis, International educator, author & blogger @ YourGlobalFamily.com.

"*Make Money on Medium* is an insightful dive into the keys for success in writing and publishing on Medium. It can get a beginner off to a jumpstart, and help experienced writers increase their audience penetration. I strongly recommend anyone wishing to write successfully on Medium to read it immediately. Nicole Akers is a real Medium Guru having written on Medium, created Publishous as one of the leading Medium publishers and PublishousNow.com, an online magazine with over 1.5 million monthly views."

– Randy Shingler, essayist, poet, haiku adventurer, author of *Tranquil Freedom, A Poetic Journey* and over 1500 pieces published on Medium.

"*Make Money on Medium* is the guide I wish I had years ago. It is down-to-earth, helpful and super encouraging. I'd recommend this book to all writers so they can start making money on Medium!"

– Jim Woods author of Ready Aim Fire

"Nicole Akers has written the definitive guide to making money on Medium. Not only is she an author, owner of a Medium publication and all-around great human being, but she is also willing to share her knowledge of the Medium platform in this book.

"*Make Money on Medium* is the book I wish I had when I started writing on Medium. She delivers the nuts and bolts of successful writing on Medium and she does it in a way that makes you want to stop reading her book and get started writing immediately. My advice is "don't do that."

Her book delivers exactly what you need to know in exactly the order you need to do it in and you don't want to make a mistake by skipping any of her advice.

Get this book now. Don't wait, don't think twice, just get it. It will save you time and energy and will make your entry into the Medium platform easy and effective."
    – Michael Shook: plainspoken author, publisher, and speaker

Make Money on Medium

Build Your Audience & Grow Your
Income with Medium.com

Nicole Akers

Published through Amazon/Kindle, in the United States of America
410 Terry Ave.
North, Seattle, WA, 98109-5210

First printing, 2019.

Nicole Akers
www.PublishousNow.com

For writers everywhere, for my family who offered unending support, and for all my high school friends who signed my yearbook saying they knew I would be a published author.

Table of Contents

Prologue

Congratulations! You've made the first step toward making money by writing on Medium.com by purchasing this book. Now, make sure you solidify your success by following through and actually reading this book.

All of it.

Cover to cover.

Because you are reading this book, I'm going to guess that you are one of several kinds of people. I'm going to guess that you're:

A) A budding writer who is looking to hone his /her craft and is looking for a new and exciting place to find an audience and engage in community with other writers. Or,

B) An experienced writer who wants to challenge her/himself by writing alongside other top-level writers who can (you see where this is going) write to more skilled writers, not necessarily because that's your audience (although it might be), but because you want the McNoobertons to see the potential for this to be a place to become pros.

C) A writer who is disciplined and shows up daily. You write every single day and publish content often.
D) A writer whose well runs dry of inspiration often. Writing is always on your mind, but you struggle to put pen to paper to show the world the thoughts swirling in your head.

The great news is that no matter which group you fall into - or if I totally missed my guess and you don't fall squarely into any of those groups - this book is for you. I will walk you through how you can grow as a writer - both in skill and in audience size - and how to make money doing it.

How do I know I can do this for you?

Because I've done it for me.

What you hold in your hands is the distilled knowledge I've gathered from years of writing on Medium.com and honing my craft (find and follow me at medium.com/@nicolesincredible), plus things I've learned from trial and error (and error, and error...) from not only growing my personal following but also from creating one of the top publications on Medium with over 11,000 followers in just over a year.

You may be one of the followers of Publishous (medium.com/publishous) [if you are, thank you; if you're not, come check us out]. We've grown to become one of the top publications (or pubs for short) by helping up-and-coming writers get noticed. As the founder and publisher, I have read - literally - thousands of stories and have picked up no shortage of tips on how to help writers like you make the most out of this powerful writing community.

Are you ready to build your audience and grow your income?

Great! Let's do this!

Tell you what...

Let me do something more for you before we dive in. Because you've decided to read the Prologue and not skip it like most people, I'll give you a gift.

That's right, a gift for just following through and reading the book you bought to read.

Since you've shown yourself to be extraordinary, I know you're the kind of person I want to connect with. So reach out to me www.publishousnow.com/medium-checklist/ and I'll give you a checklist that will jumpstart your success.

Introduction: What does Medium Have to do with Writers?

Isn't medium for artists and psychics? Those kinds of mediums are different. This Medium is for writers.

Medium.com was started in 2012 by Evan Williams. In case you're not familiar with his name, you'll certainly be familiar with his work - he was the one who got this whole online-writing-as-a-thing thing started when he started Blogger in 1999. After he sold that to Google in 2003, he made microblogging the next big thing by creating Twitter in 2006. You're probably picking up on a theme here - this guy created stuff that quickly entered the mainstream and became a fixture in popular society.

As a writer, you've found your Golden Ticket. (And for better or worse you didn't even have to eat any Willy Wonka chocolate bars to get it. Yay for your waistline. Boo for your tastebuds.)

Consider this your behind-the-scenes tour of the chocolate factory - minus the creepy Oompa Loompas.

You are about to get a look at how you can use Medium to hone your writing, find - and engage - an audience, and even make money doing what you love.

How's that for a value proposition?

Before we get too far in, let's start with an introduction to this powerful writing community.

MEDIUM.COM

Medium is a social media platform that revolves around the written word and the thoughts that go into it. It is built in such a way that readers and writers get to socialize with each other about what they've read and/or written and how they feel about it.

Medium calls itself a place to read and write big ideas and important stories. Writers know it's a place to get noticed and make money for their craft. That's great, unless you don't know how to get started on the platform.

Medium is for anyone who has long-form thought (i.e. more than the 280 characters, or so). On Medium, you get the opportunity to tell stories. It's a place to bring your ideas for others to engage with them.

A lot of people have created their path to the red carpet "stardom" by getting started on Medium. Celebrities write on Medium as a creative outlet for writing they don't want to share in other places.

They use it as a diary of sorts to share thoughts, test ideas, and pilot new content. It's not just a place for the celebs to dress up; it's a place with a low bar of entry, where everyone can find success.

Dream out loud and share your real-life thoughts, ideas, and words. Make it anything you want it to be.

Step outside yourself and pretend it's not just a life for celebrities but a life meant for you.
There are other "celebrities" on Medium, ones who aren't household names. You know, the ones with a zillion followers who are killing it in their circles, but whom you've probably never heard of. They are "famous" in their own ways and they are making a lot of money. People like:

- Tom Kuegler (@tomkuegler)
- Ben Hardy (@benjaminhardy)
- Anthony Moore (@anthony_moore)
- Ayodeji Awosika (@Chef_BoyarDEJI).

You don't have to be a NY Times bestselling author to be a successful writer.

The Internet has created the ability for average Joes and Janes to become celebrities.

Think about it.

Want to be a TV star? You can be. Start a TV station by creating an account on YouTube and recording a video.

Want to be a radio personality? You can be. Anyone can create a radio program by starting a podcast with iTunes or Stitcher.

What about you?

Have you ever dreamed of writing for a leading newspaper?

Dreamed of seeing your byline among the likes of award-winning authors?

What if you could write on the same website as the likes of Hillary Clinton, Gary Vaynerchuck, and Biz Stone? Would you be interested?

Disclaimer: Not advocating for or against any political opinion. Please don't miss the point that Medium is a place where figureheads share their thoughts, and it's easy to share the same platform with them and engage with them and their thoughts.

Would you be interested if I said you could get paid for it?

What would you say if I told you you could do exactly that - right now?

I hope you would say, "Sign me up!"

I'm about to help you do just that.

Together we'll build your audience, and you'll be able to get paid to write.

Try on the celebrity life, the Italian suit, the glamorous gown. Sip the fine wine. Grind the coffee beans and brew the first cup of the day. Have a second cup and drink up the stuff dreams are made of. Roll it around on your palate and savor the experience; relish it like the scent of clean air after it rains. Inhale slowly as if in a botanical garden, and let yourself live the dream you've reserved for others.

Next, slowly come back into the present with those possibilities at the forefront of your mind. This is real-life, not a fairy tale, and a real possibility for you.

We give celebrities too much credit, thinking it's a life reserved for someone else, but it's a life we can live too. We've neglected the possibilities for too long. It's time to stop living in our dreams and step into real life potential.

You follow your favorite kind of celebrity. We all do. It's human nature.
I want to be...
Popular like the Kardashians, sophisticated like Tom Brokaw, entertained by singers like Adam Levine, washed in the wisdom of Morgan Freeman, laugh with the humor of Betty White,...

Those celebs aren't on Medium.

We check in on people who we believe have already succeeded in living the dream.

These celebrities ARE writing on Medium:
- Gary Vaynerchuck (@garyvee)
- Ev Williams (@ev)
- Hillary Clinton (@HillaryClinton)
- Tim O'Reilly (@timoreilly)
- Marc Andreessen (@pmarca on)
- M.G. Siegler (@mgsiegler)
- Julie Zhou (@joulee)
- Larry Kim (@larrykim)
- Jon Acuff (@jon_acuff)
- James Altucher (@jaltucher)
- Jason Fried (@jasonfried).

You can live this life.

Here's an example of where a high-profile person has used Medium effectively. Amazon CEO Jeff Bezos (@jeffreypbezos) wrote about his affair on Medium. To prevent being blackmailed, he broke the story of how he betrayed his wife. It's a modern-day soap opera with a mix of love, lust, money, politics, bribery, payouts, threats, and selfies. Bezos was threatened that personal, intimate photos would be published if he didn't act in a particular way. Instead of succumbing to the threat, he broke the story himself.

Medium is social media for writers to test content of everything. It's a tool to be used in a variety of ways. I haven't found many stories with such impact as Mr. Bezos' story. Bezos clearly used Medium as a tool. Whatever you want to write about has a place on Medium.

All content has a home on Medium, even if it is published to your personal profile. It's a place to tell stories that make an impact. Tell stories that matter; maybe they are non-fiction, personal stories, or maybe they are fiction.

It doesn't matter what you write about; every topic has a home on Medium.

Medium is the place for anyone to write about anything.

Your writer friends are on Medium.

They keep telling you that you need to be there too. You half-heartedly started an account, and threw together a profile, but you're not sure what to do next.

Sound like you?

You're not alone.

Maybe you stumbled across Medium while conducting a search for art supplies or trying to find a psychic. Or you've heard about Medium from your writer friends and decided it's time for you to get noticed like others have. You can go in any direction, and the potential is endless.

But you need to know how to dance across Medium if your writing is going to get noticed. It's time to dress your writing in a way that makes it stand out on this platform.

You have some decisions to make as to how to proceed on Medium, and since you've accepted the invitation, you are going to the ball. It's time to dance with each keystroke and make your writing come alive. It's time to dress your writing in a way that helps it get noticed on Medium. Here is your chance to walk the red carpet.

LIKE A BLOG, BUT BETTER

Having a blog means you also have site maintenance and a host of technical tools and expenses like your domain and website hosting. If you're not technically savvy, this may be a hang up. Blogging on Medium eliminates all of these needs and headaches. You have the opportunity to focus on your writing and publish stories quickly and with ease. Some readers just breathed a sigh of relief. Others just said, "Wait a minute…"

"If I don't have a blog then I can't directly talk to an audience and solve their problems or potentially sell books/courses/fill in the blank…"

Medium has the potential to change the future of blogging. The Medium Partner Program offers people a basic income for being creative.

And that's a good thing!

Especially if you're a new writer who wants to see revenue from your efforts quickly. Seasoned writers are making a full-time income on this platform. You can make a little income while honing your skills or go whole hog and make a full-time income here without pursuing traditional freelance channels. You can do anything you set your mind to do. We'll cover the Medium Partner Program in Chapter 8.

For now, you need basics. In dance, you need the box step and the two-step before you get to the tango, the cha-cha-cha, the rumba. You get the idea. We'll get there, but first you need to decide what your goals are. Largely, your decisions involve two categories:

- 1. Do you want to promote yourself and your writing, i.e. get noticed?

Or

- 2. Do you want to make money with your writing on this platform, which may involve a larger business idea and using Medium as the doorway to take people somewhere else?

Some of the same basics are necessary for both categories.

WHAT IF I'M AN "AND", NOT AN "OR"?

Ah, I like this about you. You're atypical in a good way. You want to stand out. Conformity is not your strong suit. Being a wallflower in work or social engagements is not your "thing". This energy can lend itself to your success. If too prideful it can also be your hubris, but we're going to put that momentum to work for good. You don't want to *just* promote your writing. You don't want to *just* make money; you want something more. You want to promote yourself "and" make money with your writing. You're ambitious. Good for you! You're going places. It is possible to do both, but not on day one. In the early days, you're probably following one path or the other while you develop the foundational basics.

DECISIONS

It's decision time.

Do you hear the Final Jeopardy music playing?

What are your decisions and how will you get started?

Take a moment to record your goals so you can keep them in mind as we move forward.

The first thing you need to do is set up your profile.

Ch: 1 How to Create Your Profile to Get Attention

If you're brand new to Medium, you need to set up your account. The way you log into Medium depends on if you are using mobile or desktop. Once you are set up you won't see this prompt again. Decide if you will sign in using Facebook or Google.

On a computer desktop it looks like this:

On mobile it looks like this:

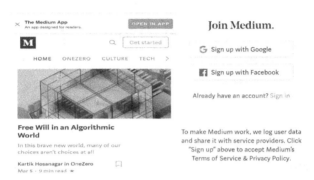

You'll receive a verification email; you must verify to create your account. Nothing we do online is absent of cookies and some kind of tracking for personal viewing preferences and marketing potential. The same is true here. You'll need to pick a few top people and publications to follow. Medium tailors what you see based on these selections. These people will appear in your "feed", and you will see the stories they publish. You'll want to gain followers, too. Hacks are coming later for you to gain followers, but for now just follow some people you know, and ask them to follow you back. Strangers may think this is rude, so just use this method for people you actually know who won't mind hearing from you in this way.

I hope you'll follow me (medium.com/@nicolesincredible) and reach out.

If you are a good fit for Publishous you might apply to write with us. Follow: medium.com/publishous and publishousnow.com/. We promote our writers, syndicate across the website and various social media platforms and provide editing and website development options.

First, you need to decide what you'll call yourself.

PICK A USERNAME

You will need to add your email address, name, and user name, which consists of up to 25 characters. Heed a caution here to choose a username you will use for an indefinite amount of time. Until very recently, you could not change your username without dissociation of everything you've published up to that point. Choosing a good username from the start is still important because that is how people get to know you as you are building your following.

Today we think we will keep our current website and last name, but life happens and things change. Pick a username that will outlast life changes. This will be your profile: https://medium.com/username.

When I started my account I chose @nicolesincredible

(medium.com/@nicolesincredible). Appreciate your follow. This is not the username I would choose today. Now I can change my username and tags across Medium will redirect, but any links to my profile outside Medium will not redirect.

My username is a source of frustration for people who want to tag me in their stories. They aren't able to tag me easily. They have to visit my profile and copy the suffix extension of the profile address to tag me in their stories. I'll stick with the incredible name and work out a marketing angle, but learn from my lesson: I would not choose this name today.

Choose your name carefully.

You probably don't want to use Mom's sweet nickname for you as she pinches your cheeks, unless you don't mind sharing it with the world. A pet nickname might be okay, but pets die and marriages fail. Names change. You can change your Medium profile name too, but I don't recommend it. For the most part, you'll want to pick a username that you will want to have in the future.

BIOGRAPHY

Enter a biography of up to 160 characters. Carefully craft this to be a powerful representation of what you want others to know about you. This is the place to market yourself and/or make your profile memorable. It may include a website. This is one of the preferred places to share your website if you have one. If you don't have a website you have more room to share about yourself. If you do have a website you're remiss by not adding it to your profile. It's an easy click-through opportunity for those who enjoy your writing to easily arrive at your domain.

For those looking to make money, this is the place to define yourself and your genre. You can draw your readers in - make readers want to clap for and interact with you. Your biography can easily be changed in the future with no adverse effects.

IMAGE

Add an image. Notice I didn't say you have the opportunity to add an image. You do have the opportunity to add an image, but, in my humble opinion, you don't appear serious about being on this platform unless you have an image. It's okay if you are not fond of showing your face. Add a logo or image from your website. Make something creative on a free design website like Canva. Add a picture of your pet, if necessary.

Add an image so that you don't look like a gray ghost on this platform. You'll see profiles with this image. You don't want to be one of them. Most have very few followers. Every once in a while you'll find a gray ghost person with a surprising number of followers, but unless you want to shout, "Hey, I'm a newbie here" don't look like this:

See how generic that looks? If your profile is the equivalent to a handshake introduction, you want to be open and inviting. A gray ghost turns people off. When I add writers to my publication and view their profile, I want to see who they are and what they write about. Seeing a gray ghost is a deterrent. I'm less interested in people who don't appear to make a strong positive statement about being here.

If you don't have a good picture available, you can capture an image straight from the camera on your computer or device. Your profile picture can be changed at any time with ease and no adverse effects.

You want to make a positive impression and help people identify with your writing. The best way to do that is to see your face. So what if you don't like pictures of yourself? You've got a lot to say, so let people know who's talking.

CONNECT YOUR SOCIAL ACCOUNTS

You can connect your Facebook and Twitter accounts, and I suggest you do. You also have the opportunity to share to those profiles. I don't enjoy automatic sharing across my profiles unless I can craft the posts and tag the author as well as using hashtags, so I don't generally use these options, but there's a huge benefit you're missing out on if you do not connect your social accounts.

Your profile will include links to your Facebook and Twitter pages if those accounts are connected to your Medium account.

Better yet, you are building up your Medium audience instantly and with no additional effort. A follow on those other platforms is a follow on Medium too, if the follower is on Medium. That's a bonus you don't want to miss out on. There is a certain amount of customization available. Go through the settings to manage what kind of emails you receive and how often you receive them.

Once you learn how things work on Medium, you may want to become a member so you can get paid for your work. Writing is good and getting paid for what you love to do is even better. Consider becoming a partner so you can read unlimited stories and support other writers who are also members. We'll go into the MPP--Medium Partner Program--in depth in chapter 8. It involves strategy and list building, too, if that's your thing, but first become familiar with the basics.

Ch 2: Get the Basics for Unprecedented Success

Now that you've created your account and set up your profile, you need to know the basics about how things work around here.

This is where you'll learn the ropes and how to build a foundation on them.

During your first month on Medium, you're going to be building your presence in the community. Don't be surprised if your early work isn't getting much attention right away. This time is growing you in ways you can't see or measure by practicing your craft and engaging with others. You're establishing consistency and writing.

If you are new to Medium, you probably need to spend time familiarizing yourself with what happens here: that is, to understand what others are doing on this platform--what works and what doesn't. It's a good idea to follow some of the big shots because they are already successful on this platform.

Model yourself after them. (Read *emulate*, not *steal*.)

To a certain extent, writers have similar ideas. The good ones emulate ideas that work by making them their own. They don't steal; they make a thought their own through tweaking, testing, and adding their own personality.

Model their behaviors, their formatting, their stylistic components and put those elements to work with your personality and in your writing.

You have to do you if you're to be believable.

"Be yourself; everyone else is already taken." - Unknown

Don't fake them. Make you.

Please don't hear, "Go steal from the best." Please do hear *borrow the ideas that work for them and put them to work for you.*

While you're studying the best and brightest, you need to be working, too.

What should I be working on?

Glad you asked.

Unless you're a total pantser (i.e. one who enjoys flying by the seat of her/his pants versus having to plot out every next step), it means that you need to spend some time getting familiar with this platform.

Quick side note: this is no judgement of pantsers. I am one of you. Fist bumps to the pantsers. I get an idea and a brief plan in my head then go after it. That's how we do it, yes? We fine-tune as we act.

Medium is a forgiving platform. You can test ideas. If there's something you want to write about - do it. If you're passionate about more than one topic while you're finding your voice and your audience on this platform, write to explore who you are, how your ideas perform, and who responds to them. Gauge what you do next based on how people interact with your stories.

If you receive a handful of comments and highlights you may assume your piece resonated with a group of people who may become your audience. Interaction, whether positive or negative, means you struck a chord. Maybe this is a topic you want to keep writing about. If something doesn't work or work well, it might just need to be tweaked. Note what you learn here. It's valuable.

If you're not a pantser, you're probably a planner. Some of you will study this platform for months before you write your first story. Either way is okay.

READ

Read, read, read. Some of you will read morning, noon, and night, until your eyes are bloodshot and weary, to find the stories and topics you like to read. You'll write an abundance of stories to learn first-hand what works for you and what does not. You'll have written a book-worth of content and have some intel to know what works. You'll painstakingly pour yourself over stats.

Others will learn by reading and seeing what works for other writers.

Either way is okay, and both are valuable.

ENGAGEMENT

Engagement is an important part of the platform. The way you engage across the platform can help you earn money if you lock pieces through the Medium Partner Program, but it's also important for writers who aren't members. It's a way of gauging whether or not writers like your work. Is that too much too early? Don't worry; there's a whole section on the Medium Partner Program (MPP) in chapter 8.

You'll find engagement throughout the Medium help pages used a variety of ways, but what it really measures is the way you interact with a piece. Interaction is important, and some interaction is more valuable than others. Giving applause is simple but the weakest form of engagement.

You'll want to read and comment on others' stories, too. When you write a comment, your response becomes its own story that's posted on your profile; someone can clap for and respond to your comment. The engagement measurement is ever-changing and the algorithms change, too, but "engagement", according to Medium guidelines, is three-fold. It involves applause, highlights, and comments. These components gauge how likeable your piece is.

Applause/Claps

Maybe you're asking yourself how to engage with stories on Medium. You engage by giving applause, highlighting a portion of text that is impactful, or commenting on a story. If you think you're issuing claps for the posts you like, your impression is different than what the founder intended. The founder intended for us to issue applause.

Consider a performance, a speech, and a concert. You give applause--not claps--based on how you much you enjoy a performance. Applause... Claps... Does it matter? They are the same thing, right? If you really enjoy a performance you might clap until your hands hurt. It's the same on Medium. You issue applause to the degree you feel moved by the story.   Applause happens on a scale of 1-50. You applaud based on how much you like the story. There are a lot of theories behind how to "clap". I'll leave it up to you how to clap and share the mechanics of issuing applause.

You'll see a vertical bar like this to the left of each story.

Click the hand up to 50 times to issue applause. Also notice the options to bookmark the piece to read it later, Tweet a link of the piece, or share it on Facebook,

People get excited when they think you are telling them how to "clap". I read a parody once about

Publishous

Discover the best up and coming writers. You'll say you knew them when.

Owner ∨

 647

the psycho-analysis of a person based on the applause he gives others. It covered everything from clapping 50 times for friends to applauding once, as though through tightened butt cheeks, like you had to squeeze to keep too many claps from falling out.

If you clap 50 times for all your buddies on share threads in writer groups you are weakening the value of your applause. And, if you clap once, you're probably making your friends mad. If you're sending one little clap it's kind of like saying, "I didn't have time to read your piece, but I'm here" or "I read your piece and it sucks".

Most people give applause based on a scale they have set for themselves. As a pub owner, I touch a lot of stories each day. I run out of claps often because there is a limit to how many pieces a person can applaud for in a 24 hour period. I add applause to boost the writers who publish with us, but some days I've met my quota and run out. I clap based on a scale I've developed for writer friends, people who publish through the pub, how the piece affects me, and whether or not it is a member piece.

You have to decide what works for you.

WRITE STORIES

When you're comfortable with how the platform works, you're ready to write stories, or maybe you've been publishing stories while you've been learning the basics. It's time to write stories: long stories, short, stories, fiction stories, life lessons, technology: there are many different genres on Medium. If you can't find a publication that accepts anything you want to write about, then you may want to start one for yourself. If you are a blogger, a *story* is synonymous with a blog post. A story is the method by which you publish your work on Medium. It's a piece of writing you share across the platform. When you publish a piece of writing, you are publishing your story to share with the world.

More on how to get people to read what you've written and how to format your stories in the coming chapters.

GET SUPPORT

Some say you've got to find your tribe. It's really about a sense of closeness and support. The word itself is derived from the Native American culture and the unity they developed, a dependence on one another to meet basic survival needs. Today the word is antiquated and overused.

However you choose to do it, you need to connect with other writers who are doing the same thing--writing. You need to yoke together with people who are doing the same thing, because some people will never understand "that blogging thing" and how it makes money.

Maybe your family doesn't understand, but a writer will empathize with what you are going through and be able to offer encouragement. Find a group of writers who is active and understands a writer's life.

Are you ready?

Let's explore details that get people to read what you've written.

Ch 3: How to Get People to Read What You've Written

Write stories that offer value and publish them consistently. When you're new to the platform you want to publish once a week, at bare minimum. Ideally, you want to publish at least 2-3 times a week. If this feels like a lot of work at first, it is, and it's worth the effort. You'll wrestle with whether to publish shorter pieces often or to publish lengthier content less frequently and what mix is appropriate based on the time you have available to invest.

Here's a secret. Everyone else wrestles with the same thing. To a degree, you have to decide what works for you. The more you practice the better your writing becomes and the more quickly you complete the "work".

How do you write stories that matter?

This is what you've been waiting for.

Tom Petty and the Heartbreakers will say, "The waiting is the hardest part."

Violet Fane is credited with saying, "Good things come to those who wait".

Do you know that is not the full quote?

"Good things come to those who wait but only the things left by those who hustle," is the full quote. I'm not a fan of hustling all the time. You'll wear yourself out and take yourself out of the game in your prime. That's a whole other story.

So far you've:
- Started your account
- Set up your profile in a meaningful way, including a website, if applicable
- Learned some basics about how the platform works
- Learned how to applaud for stories

If you've hustled through the set-up of your Medium account and done it well, then good for you!!

LEGALESE

Let's get the legalese out of the way. Did you just yawn? It's as simple and as quick as I can make it. Perhaps a little boring, but necessary. Hang with me for a minute. We'll rip off the band-aid and move on quickly.

Writers often wonder: *who owns my writing?*

You do.

It's throughout Medium's published guidelines that you own the rights to the material you publish on Medium. Some pubs say otherwise, but this is not in accordance with Medium guidelines. Some pubs ask for a time frame of exclusivity before republishing. If there's a reason you can't comply with the request, contact your pub to discuss. If you've been offered a book deal and it's become necessary to take down your content from other areas, contact your pub. They'll probably celebrate with you. Some pubs say if you remove your content, i.e. "pull a piece", as a repeat occurrence, they will remove you as a writer, and it stands to reason. If the pub was instrumental in the success of your piece by its promotion and extra eyes, it may not be pleased to see pieces pulled, especially if it's patterned behavior.

You own the content and you are responsible for all the risks that come with it, including any claim that may arise as to its intellectual property and the right to publish it. You are free to publish content on Medium that you have published elsewhere, provided you have the legal right to do so. By posting content on Medium you are making assurances that you are not in violation of any other agreements you have in place.

Medium can remove any content you post for any reason and may change its terms of service at any time without prior written notice. This all makes sense. As a writer or entrepreneur, you want the freedom to make changes as you wish. Odds are good that as a company, Medium will offer upcoming changes in writing, but they are under no obligation to do so.

That wasn't so bad, now was it?

STRUCTURING YOUR STORY

Hopefully, you've taken a decent survey of what happens around here and how to participate. If so, then you're ready to take action by writing stories. Writing stories on Medium is a little different than on your blog. If you're not taking into account mobile readers, then you're losing readers before you've had a chance to gain them.

Whether you are writing for mobile eyes, or on Medium, it is important to write for scanners. Scanners are people who read your content quickly by scanning, or scrolling with the touch of a finger. They don't read every word they scan for the sake of expediency.

If that wasn't strong enough for you to change your writing style, allow me to say it this way:

YOU ARE THROWING AWAY 50% OF YOUR TRAFFIC BY NOT FORMATTING FOR MOBILE READERS.

If you have kids, some days they are drive-by-eaters who scan the meal before they decide whether or not to dive in.

It's like asking mom what's for dinner. Let's say the answer is meatloaf. You have to decide whether or not the meal is worth eating based on the answer. If you love meatloaf your mouth is probably watering.

"Yes, give me some of that; I can't wait for dinner."

If you hate meatloaf, you're wondering what else is for dinner.

You might say:
"No thanks; I'll pass."

The reader makes the same decisions based on your headlines.

HEADLINES

Your headline makes the first impression. It needs to get the reader's attention. If you don't grab their attention in the headline they will never read your story. It's that simple. You need a headline that performs or you've wasted your effort in publishing a story.

If you write clickbait headlines to garner attention, they may or may not have a place on Medium. Clickbait headlines, if you are unfamiliar with them, are headlines written with the sole purpose of getting the reader to click through to the piece. They're great for advertising but a manipulation to get the reader to click the link. Use them carefully and probably only on occasion. Simple, straight forward headlines perform best. You want a headline that is powerful or makes a bold statement. Make sure people can easily understand it.

Don't use acronyms or abbreviations that aren't commonly understood.

Do use numbers for listicles and concrete takeaways.

Make a promise. Promise to solve a common problem then deliver the solution.

Use *What, Why, How, When* in your headline. Think about receiving an invitation. You get the bullet point of what's to come, which details how we're celebrating so and so's birthday…

The headline can make or break the story.

A caution: headline analyzers can lead you toward a clickbait title. A clickbait title is content created for the purpose of getting the reader to click through the link. This may or may not involve the use of profanity. If you know that Medium favors straight forward titles then you can get a good performing straight-forward title without much trouble. There are a lot of good free ones. Here are some:

- Sharethrough
  (headlines.sharethrough.com)
- Blog Title Generator by SEOPressor
  (seopressor.com/blog-title-generator)
- HubSpots Blog Idea Generator
  (hubspot.com/blog-topic-generator)
- Title Generator by Tweak Your Biz
  (tweakyourbiz.com/title-generator)
- Portent's Content Idea Generator
  (portent.com/tools/title-maker)
- Blog Title Generator by BlogAbout
  (impactbnd.com/blog-title-generator/blogabout)
- UpWorthy Title Generator
  (upworthygenerator.com/)
- CoSchedule Headline Analyzer
  (coschedule.com/headline-analyzer)

Good headlines draw you in and solve a problem. They entertain and explain quickly. They reach a reader's source of pain and solve a problem. They get to the point rapidly and boldly.

- Use *how* or *why* to solve a problem
- Begin with a number
- Make an audacious promise, then deliver on it

Once you have a good headline, you're ready to write the story.

Let's play with headlines for the sport of it. Here we will introduce a headline, see how it scores with a headline analyzer, and learn how to improve it until it performs. I've used CoSchedule for the testing you see below. This is an example of what you can do each time you write a headline. Here we go!

What would make you want to eat meatloaf, even if you dislike it?

Something like:

How To Prepare The Most Magnificent Meatloaf You'll Ever Eat

How To Prepare The Most Magnificent Meatloaf You Ll Ever Eat

Word Balance

An analysis of the overall structure, grammar, and readability of your headline.

COMMON		27%
ever, how, ll, most, the, to, you,		
UNCOMMON		0%
Increase the number of uncommon words in your headline to improve your headline		
EMOTIONAL		36%
how to, the most,		
POWER		0%
Increase the number of power words in your headline to improve your headline		

Now we're talking. Meatloaf might be something you never want to eat, but the title is so delicious you might just try it anyway. Good titles persuade.

That actually scored pretty well with a headline analyzer, but it may be a little long for mobile users.

How To Prepare The Best Meatloaf You'll Ever Eat

How To Prepare The Best Meatloaf Youll Ever Eat

Word Balance

An analysis of the overall structure, grammar, and readability of your headline.

COMMON ever, how, the, to,		22%
UNCOMMON youll		11%
EMOTIONAL how to, the best,		22%
POWER best,		11%

HEADLINE TYPE:

How To

That's even better. Let's see if it can be improved.

How To Prepare The Best Meatloaf Ever

How To Prepare The Best Meatloaf Ever

Word Balance

An analysis of the overall structure, grammar, and readability of your headline

COMMON		28%
ever, how, the, to.		
UNCOMMON		0%
Increase the number of uncommon words in your headline to improve your headline		
EMOTIONAL		29%
how to, the best.		
POWER		14%
best		

Target a headline that performs at 80%, a fantastic performance rate. If you end up a little short, say, in the strong 70% range, you know you have a pretty good title. If you're a perfectionist, keep working it until you're happy. In the 75 and upward percentile, I rest in the comfort of a well-crafted headline and go write the story. Work the title until you are comfortable knowing you've done all you can to get readers to click through and read your story.

Choose your words carefully. Use common words to boost performance. The word "make" outperforms "prepare" with an increase of 2%.

How to Make The Best Meatloaf Ever

How To Make The Best Meatloaf Ever

Word Balance

An analysis of the overall structure, grammar, and readability of your headline

COMMON — 28%
an is, these, the, to

UNCOMMON — 0%
make

EMOTIONAL — 43%
how to make the best

POWER — 14%
best

HEADLINE TYPE:
How To

The old Journalism adage holds true: 5-7 words is about right for a title. It's a delicate balance of performance and word length. Too many words and you'll lose readers' interest.

In the early days, you may spend more time writing the title than you do writing the story. I know it sounds crazy, but it's not, and it's time worth spending.

If you're a blogger you know that it's important to add your keyword to the title. In this case, the keyword is "meatloaf". Seasoned bloggers who have independent websites know that they need good SEO for website performance. One way to improve SEO is to add your keyword to the title.

Need help writing headlines?

USE A HEADLINE ANALYZER

Sometimes you can feel a good headline. I've had headlines I thought were great and I popped them into an analyzer only to find out they sucked rocks. I still use a headline analyzer every time. It's too important to use a headline that will perform well.

Get the reader's attention in the headline and you've got them reading your story. Now you want to keep them reading.

How do you do that?

Keep reading.

GIVE SOMETHING MORE

Give readers a good introduction and a quick overview of what's coming: a reason to keep reading. What else do you have to say on the topic? You probably aren't having just meatloaf for dinner. What else are you eating? What sides? Is it meatloaf and salad? Meatloaf and broccoli?

One kid hates meat, but loads up on veggies. This is a parent's dream come true, yes? This kid will show up for dinner and eat because he loves broccoli. The other kid just wants to eat the meatloaf, hold the veggies.

Get to the point of the piece and get there early. Wait too long and you've lost your reader.

What is the point of the story? Share it quickly so the reader doesn't leave before you've ever gotten to the point. Offer the basics of the story to keep the reader interested and hold him on the page.

Don't like broccoli? That's fine; I've got salad, too.

Make sure the main idea of the story appears quickly. Give them a hook that will keep them reading.

Next, unpack the subtopics more slowly.

THE MEAT

Shall we dine? Let's sink our teeth into the meat of the subject.

We've enticed them with a great headline and given them the hook. Now it's time to deliver the main course. Bring on the meatloaf, the meat, the main point of your story. Don't let them eat cake. Thank you but no, Marie Antoinette; it's not time for dessert. Let them eat meat. Give them content they can sink their teeth into.

It's time for the main idea of the story. I'm assuming you're already a writer and know what you want to say. I'm not touching on content generation here, assuming you already have content to share.

USE THE IMPORT TOOL

What if you've written something on your blog and want to share it on Medium too? Medium has a tool to import work from your blog. It's clunky and doesn't always hold the form of the original post, but it carries a wee bit of code at the end to share the original source of where the work is published.

From your profile, drop down to stories → import a story.

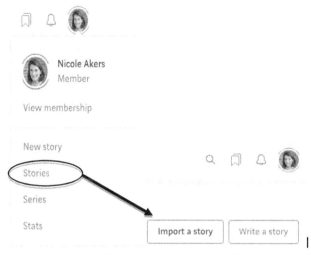

I nsert a website address from the original source of publication, which is probably your blog.

See your story on Medium

Import a story from anywhere on the internet to publish on your Medium account.

Enter a link to your blog post/article/story/manifesto to import and share it on Medium.

http://www.yoursite.org/your-post

You will have a chance to edit it before making it public.

Import

Please only import content that you own.

It is easy to bring a post from your blog into a story on Medium, but the formatting doesn't always hold and sometimes chunks of text get omitted. A thorough read of your content is necessary before publishing. The original date of publishing is added to the bottom of the story, so it will fall down the publication page to the original publication date.

Stories are shown on your profile in chronological order, by the date they were written, unless you pin a piece to the top of your profile, in which case it works just like Facebook or Twitter, where it stays on the top.

Remember the Google favor we talked about earlier?

If you want your Medium piece to perform, it needs to be connected to the original place it was published on the internet. Again, that's probably your blog. Medium developers seamlessly integrated the connection when using the import tool. You don't have to do anything. The import tool does it for you. The note appears as originally published on the name of your blog on the date it was published.

There are a lot of different theories about whether to publish on your blog first or publish on Medium first. I've done both and I'm not sure it matters. It is good to leave some distance between one kind of publishing to another. Some suggest a week; others say a few days.

You have to decide what is right for you. If you want original content to go out on your blog then you would post there and import to Medium via the import tool. Copy and paste is not advisable because the piece of code to connect the piece from your blog to Medium is not added.

Some people like to give the first published piece to their blog audience. Others like to debut the content on Medium and refine it based on comments and performance. They improve the content before publishing to their blog so that their subscribers receive the best, most refined content.

There isn't a right or wrong answer here. It is personal preference. The big takeaway is if you choose to import, using the import tool is key so that the connection is made to the original published piece. Google's algorithms change, but it is important to connect the piece to the original source of publication, the first published location, for Google favor.

Regardless, whether you are writing a new story or importing from your blog, you still want to do what I talk about next.

USE SMALL BLOCKS OF TEXT

Notice what I didn't say: I didn't say minimize your content. DO entertain everything you want your story to be. Use all the vivid description and detail you can add for great storytelling, but break it up into small blocks of text, which doesn't mean thinking small. It means think spaciously.

I've heard people argue against this point and I laugh every time. This isn't optional. The web isn't going away. If you don't format for mobile users people are not going to read your words.

Use different types of subheadings as you go deeper. Introduce a list by using bullet points or a numbered list like this:

- H1 Title
- H2 Main Point
- H3 Subpoint

Subheadings go to H6, but there's rarely a reason to use all of them. If you're using H1-H3 you are using subheadings effectively.

Subheadings are simplified on Medium. Big "T" or small "t". Big "T" is for your main title and subheadings get the small "t" selection.

Don't forget to proofread your work and use good grammar. Use spell check, Grammarly, Hemingway, or other free resources to edit your work. Content is still king. Write about topics people like to read and present it with whitespace, using good grammar, and as professionally edited as possible.

END WITH A CTA

A call to action (CTA) is how you end your story. Leave one thing in their minds that you want them to do next. This is like dessert. It's the cherry on top of the sundae. You'll see some CTAs that are as long as the entire story, or longer. That's not what you're going for here. A CTA is short, concise, and powerful.

Ex: *Want more stories like this? These are related.* Add a backlink to some of your other stories.

Ex: *For ongoing encouragement visit me on my website.*

Ex: *Recall a time you were filled with anxiety and how you overcame.*

Ex: *If you were in this situation what would you do?*

If your piece is not locked, you may ask for applause if the reader enjoyed the story. Or ask them to leave a comment.

Ex: *Like what you've read? Give me some applause by clicking on the hand up to 50 times.*
Ex: *If you were in this situation, what would you do? Tell me in the comments below.*

Don't leave the story without bringing the reader into it with you. If it's a life lesson you've learned either through pain or joy, make the lesson come alive with storytelling that will make the reader hurt or rejoice with you. Make the story relate to them.

They don't care about you as much as they care about how you relate to them and what feelings and emotions come out as they read your words.

Leave them thinking about how the story impacts them.

These elements cover how to format your text, but there's something else you need to do. No restaurant sells food without pretty food pictures. Every story needs a pretty picture like the one that made your mouth water when you pause here to eat...I mean read. Add a powerful, featured image to every story right at the top, under your title.

ADD IMAGES

A good book needs a pretty picture. So does your story. Don't publish a story without a picture or graphic.

As you read you'll notice the same pictures popping up over and over again. No two book covers are the same, but Medium is different in this regard and it's with good reason. It's because you can't use just any image you find around the web. If you're a blogger you already know this, but if you don't have a website you may not know that you can be fined for using images without permission.

You probably won't be fined as an individual. More than likely you will be contacted and asked to remove a specific graphic from your website. If you do so quickly, the problem disappears. If you publish with publications you're opening them up to fines on your behalf. I don't know a single pub who will take this risk for you. More than likely they just won't publish your piece or will give you an opportunity to replace your image.

What kind of images should you add?

Use CC (Creative Commons) license photos or graphics and cite them appropriately every time. If you are using your own picture, then note yourself as the photographer.

It is interesting to note that the CC website issues a disclaimer: In short, what CC says is trust but verify. Odds are that you will never be sued, but be aware that if you use an image the copyright owner wants taken down, you need to comply. The big companies, Disney, for example, have bots trolling nonstop, looking for their images so they can request images used without consent be taken down.

If you are in doubt about whether or not the image is CC, then don't use the image. A public cited image is not an appropriate image to use and could result in fines.

Websites that offer free images for commercial or business use have these traits in common:
1. They offer images without an exchange of money
2. They state the image is Creative Commons or is royalty free

There are plenty of websites that offer CC graphics. This is by no means an exhaustive list:

- Unsplash
- PublicDomainPictures
- Pixabay
- Pexels
- 1 Million Free Pictures
- New Old Stock
- Flickr
- Wikimedia.org

Add a royalty-free graphic to each story for appeal. If your post is long enough, it may be useful to add a graphic in the middle or at the end.

You can search for your own graphic independently or use Medium's integrated picture tool with Unsplash by using the "+", magnifying glass, and entering a keyword to see   picture   options.

I've shown the process above the title, but you can also use the integration tool throughout your   writing.

writing

Select one of those graphics for a writing topic and it will magically appear in your document.

When you've written a great title, used white space, given a hook, introduced the topic, unpacked the headings and subpoints, checked your spelling and grammar and ended with a call to action, you've served a seven-course meal that your reader will want to eat and delivered elements to make it perform well.

Once you've created or imported the text and added a graphic, it needs to be formatted.

How should I format my work?

Glad you asked. We'll cover that in depth next.

Ch 4: How to Format Your Story for Outstanding Readership

We briefly mentioned mobile users and that your stories should have short paragraphs or be chunked. Paragraphs should be about 4-5 lines in length. If you don't break up your work into small passages, you're losing your readers.

When a mobile reader sees words, words, words, he will click away. It's like the noise of Charlie Brown's teacher speaking, but it's visual noise; too much text without breaks and pictures is a good way to cause a reader to click away before he's read your story. He doesn't want to see this:

Source: Photo by Lorenzo from Pexels

His mind will glaze over and there's not a snowball's chance in you-know-where he's staying around to read your story. Gone. He'll be on to a different story and never look back.

Your story needs to be attractive to keep him on the page.
In order to be successful at this, you need to entertain him not just with your words, but visually with your words on the page.

Pexels

Never mind that it's German. Enjoy the read if you are fluent in German, but if it's a foreign language you cannot comprehend, enjoy the formatting. Just look at the text. It's eye-appealing. It has headings, subheadings, bullet points, pull-out quotes... It's pretty to look at and will hold interest on mobile. You don't want the reader to click away because TLDR (Too Long Didn't Read). With the scroll of a finger, he'll scan the piece. It's unlikely he'll read every word, but he won't read any of your words unless you break up your blocks of text.

How should I format my work?

Besides short paragraphs, there are other things you want to do.

The title gets a big T for formatting purposes. It's the  most effective thing on the page so make it large.

USE WHITESPACE

White space is your friend when formatting for mobile readership. It's easy to do, too. Many times I find myself hitting enter a lot more. If you think the way you would send a text, omitting the shorthand, you're on the right track. It doesn't only mean chunking your text. It also means using sentence fragments for effect.

Using sentence fragments doesn't mean using bad or improper grammar. It means, on occasion, using a fragment to punctuate a point. Sometimes it's effective to write like a person speaks. Use fragments well and don't overdo them.

If you've made a point that bears repeating, you can say it a different way as a pull-out quote for impact. It's a good way to deepen the point, earn highlights, and be effective on mobile simultaneously.

It's easy to format a pull-out quote. Just highlight the text you want to stand out then click twice on the ' " '. When you do, this is what your text will look like.

Kill your darlings, kill your darlings, even when it breaks your egocentric little scribbler's heart, kill your darlings. — Stephen King

The text stands out as impactful and naturally introduces whitespace.

Equally as important is to use headings, subheadings, and bulleted or numbered lists. Let's talk some more about that right now.

SUBHEADINGS

It's no coincidence that Subheads is a subhead in the text. You already have a great title (or heading), but subheads are different. They are a little smaller, usually H2 or H3 if you're a blogger. They break up the text and introduce your next point. They also naturally add whitespace. On Medium, subheads get at least a small t. Some suggest to give them a big T, too.

USE SIMPLE WORDS

This doesn't mean sacrifice content. It means to cut out the fluff. Write with simple thoughts that aren't confusing or use big words. It's not a chance to show off your IQ by using as many large words as possible. Use simple words that are to the point. Readers, especially mobile readers, want a smooth experience that doesn't have them seeking Google for a definition. If they have to go look up a word, it's possible they won't return to finish your story.

Adding too many big or unnecessary words is like adding winter weight. It holds you back. Stay lean. Delete words like:
- really
- too
- very
- that (in most cases)
- anyways
- so
- I think
- actually

And simplify common expressions like:
- at this point in time = now
- a majority of = most
- on account of = because
- fewer in number = fewer
- in my opinion = I think
- large numbers of = many

Simple, straight-forward, to the point writing is key. Cut the fluff.

Notice I added those fluff words in a bulleted list. It is helpful to add content in a bulleted list for eye appeal, and it adds additional while space naturally, a double bonus.

STYLING

Styling is different; pull out quotes don't get quotation marks. They get the double click quote, which pulls them out and makes them italicized, as in the picture above.

Words used as direct quotations get the single quote, which adds them with quotation marks.

Bold and Italics are good formatting tools. Use bold sparingly and for powerful effect.These are easy to introduce. Just highlight the text you want to format and select "b" or" i", appropriately.

Italics may be used stylistically or for emphasis, sometimes for a person's internal thoughts or direct conversation. These options are available in the same way you create a pull-out quote. See pic above and choose the correct option, as applicable.

SUMMARY

Wrap up your piece with a summary, call to action, or leave the reader with a thought that causes him/her to think about doing something.

A review of points is a good way to end:

Ex: *The next time you're overly anxious, use these three tips to calm your nerves.*

Whatever your call to action, it should be short and concise. This is the one thing you want the reader to do next. Don't make it lengthy. I see a lot of CTAs that are longer than the piece itself. Don't do this. The reader doesn't want to read more about you than the content you've presented.

Ex: *What's the one thing you need to tell your kids that you thought they already knew? Say it today!*

Ex: *Want more pieces like this? Sign up and they'll come as special delivery to your inbox.*

Short. Powerful. Done.

Formatting your story includes using whitespace, headings and subheadings, simple words, pull-out quotes, and ending with a CTA. Before publishing, re-read your story to make sure it makes sense. Use these elements in every story for maximum impact.

Ch 5: How to Get, and Keep, Followers

Being on this platform is great. You've set-up your profile, added your website if applicable, attached social accounts, learned the basics of writing a good headline and how to structure your story. That's all positive momentum and a good foundation, but it's not enough. You also need followers.

What are followers?

Followers are the number of people who see your stories when you publish them. They are people who see your work in their feed as they scroll. If you aren't in writing groups for support, I strongly suggest you get connected with some quickly. In depth details of how to find them and what happens there can be found in chapter 10.

Getting 100 followers is your first milestone. Achieve that quickly and you're on your way! You've hacked a month of work to a day or two.

Are you in writing groups yet?

Go get in some good ones right now.

You can do this alone, but it's not easy. Get support from people who have been where you are and know you will get through this. You need to know you aren't alone unless you are doing this alone, and in that case, you need to allow yourself more time before you start seeing traction.

Here are some techniques to find followers and earn some yourself.

FOLLOW/UNFOLLOW

Go follow 50 people every day. Keep the ones who follow you back and unfollow the rest on a weekly basis. This can be done on mobile in about 10 minutes.

This technique gets mixed reviews and mixed results. You can go out and follow a bunch of people every day. Do this and around 10% will follow you back. I've used this technique on occasion and it is tiring, but if you're only doing this for a month, it's not too bad.

I don't unfollow near as quickly as I should. The people I follow tend to stay around for a while.

If you are ambitious, you can follow the number of people up to your daily limit: 100 at the time of this writing. When you notice your follow doesn't hold, accept that you've met your daily goal and wait until tomorrow to try again. If this is your groove, great. If not, there are other effective ways to earn followers.

FOLLOW PEOPLE WHO ENGAGE

Followers are a privilege. They don't have to stay, so treat them well. Offer outstanding content readers find entertaining and want to read, and your followers will stay. Offer weak and inconsistent content and they will leave.

- Follow people who engage
- Issue applause
- Write and respond to comments

This is a no brainer. Follow people who engage with your content. Follow up on who engages with your piece and, if you like what they write about, follow them back. You can see who applauds for your piece, so click over to their profile, read a piece that interests you and return the favor. Do this quickly by locating their top piece and engaging with it.

Remember, engagement is at least three-fold. It involves applause, highlights, and comments. Fans and reads are also important. If you're providing a read there's no tracking your engagement back to you as an individual, and your friends in writing groups will never know that you've engaged.

While reading, highlight a bit of text that makes an impact, preferably near the end so you're increasing the read rating. On your way back to the top, offer some applause and increase the fan rating, too. These are extra valuable, even more valuable than applause alone. Applause, while effective, is possibly the weakest form of engagement.

ISSUE APPLAUSE

Applause is one form of engagement, but it was the first form of engagement for issuing revenue. While still a help, it's probably the least effective form of engagement possible. But it's quick, easy, and doesn't take much time to spread engagement with a lot of people quickly. There is also a limit to the number of stories you can applaud in a 24-hour period. If you've issued healthy doses of applause and see that your applause no longer holds--your applause count stops increasing--move on to a different form of engagement and try again tomorrow (or later today). When your applause stops going up, you're done with this engagement until later.

COMMENT

This is two-fold:
1. Comment on pieces written by others.
2. Respond to comments on pieces you've written.

COMMENT ON OTHERS' WRITING

A comment is a standalone story. It shows you are active on this platform and your comments appear on your profile. Comment on five stories written by other people every day. Not just 'thanks for a great piece'. Anyone can do that in their sleep.

Offer a value comment:
Ex: Say why the piece resonates with you.
Ex: Ask if they've considered a different point of view. And then provide your point of view.
Ex: *"This reminds me of the time..."* share a short personal anecdote

Be creative.

RESPOND TO YOUR COMMENTS

If you have notifications turned on, you know when someone comments on your story. If you receive a lot of notifications it's easy to miss one. Follow up on your freshest pieces often. I find this easier than responding to notifications. Manage your comments and respond to them in bulk for productivity and time management effectiveness. Respond in a mass production assembly line fashion and rest in the assumption that you're up-to-date.

Good enough is good enough.

VIEWS, READS, AND FANS

If you are a statistician, you'll notice a view and fan rating. Both of these are important, and the ebb and flow of these seems, at times, to correspond with payout of member pieces. When these numbers are high, payouts are higher. When they are low, payout is lower. Let's visit each briefly and we'll get more in-depth later.

Views are simply the number of times your piece is viewed. Someone clicked the link and read at least a portion of your piece.

Reads are the number of times a person reads your piece; the views are measured against how far the person read for a read percentage.

Fans are people who doubly engage. They not only read your piece, but also clapped for it.

A word to the wise: Don't argue in the comments.

This is social media, and human nature may be to address your thoughts, even fight a little for your point of view. As a

1 response ▢ ⌄

Undo applause for this post

Report story

g is difficult to

nation. We have to

It's like reading a

general rule, stay away from arguing in the comments. It's an unnecessary downward spiral. Every platform has trolls who are contentious. Handle it as you will, but I suggest ignoring those comments. If tension is too much, you may report a comment. Carat down from the bottom right of a comment and report the comment if you feel it is contentious and in violation of community standards. Like this:

If you feel strongly enough about something and you can't stop yourself from speaking up, use it as a writing prompt to write a new story yourself.

Follow up with people who applaud for your piece by clicking on the hand. If you like what they write about, follow them back. You can see who applauds for your piece and how many times they clapped for it. You can click over to their profile, read a piece that interests you and return the favor.

A little follow/unfollow action while engaging in various forms will show you as an active participant on this platform. Content is king. This is true for any writer on any platform. Offer great content that people want to read and you will earn followers.

The first milestone is to achieve 100 followers quickly. Use these techniques and you'll easily have met, if not surpassed, the first milestone within 30 days.

Are you ready to engage and earn followers? Get started today!

CALL TO ACTION

Go to Medium right now.
- Follow 50 people (including @nicolesincredible [medium.com/@nicolesincredible], yes, shameless plug)
- Go to your latest piece
- Click on the hand to see who gave it applause
- Click through to their profile and applaud, highlight and/or comment on their top piece
- Wash, rinse, repeat these steps

Pat yourself on the back for your success. Really, take a moment. Breathe. Celebrate. You've come a long way.

I'm glad you took a moment to celebrate your progress.

What's that? You want even more eyes on your work?

Yeah!
Me too!

To get extra eyes on your work you need publications. Publications (or "pubs" for short) already have extra eyes. I write with pubs and have founded one myself. Write with pubs to enhance your potential before you have followers, and to continue to get a lot of views on your writing even after you've developed a following.

How do you find publications?

Turn the page and we'll explore pubs.

Ch 6: How to Find Publications and How to Treat them Right

You want eyes on your work and that's why you publish with publications. They have lots, many have thousands, of followers who would love to read what you have to say. Pubs have different followers than you do and expand your viewing audience, so you want to publish with them quickly.

The truth is this: you don't start by publishing with pubs. You start by having a strong profile and publishing quality content consistently, for a minimum of one month. You want four to five or more pieces of your best work on your profile.

Note: If you're applying to be a writer, you are sending a link as a resume of your writing. You haven't sent a story to be considered for publication until:
1. You have been accepted as a writer
2. You have sent a story to the publication queue

The pub queue is the electronic waiting room for stories that have been sent by writers to a publication. From there an editor will review your story and either publish it or send it back to you.

The publication application for Publishous asks for a link to your profile. Everything we've been doing in this book until now is what the pub wants to see at a glance. Miss these steps and you're missing opportunities to write with good publications. Make sure your profile is solid before soliciting to write with pubs.

When I look at a person's profile, I want to see who they are, what they write about, how often they write, and what skill level of writing this person presents. If a person writes once a month, I'll pass them over for a writer who writes frequently. Pubs can accept a limited number of writers into their writer bank, so they want the best ones who write often. If you haven't published a story, you're going to get the canned response: "You're not a good fit for us. Best!" If you've only published one story, I'm not interested until you have established consistency.

The more full my writer bank is, the more stringent my criteria becomes. I'd like to see more than a month of content. I want to know this is not a fad for you. Think about it this way: In January, everyone who wants to get in shape promises to go to the gym, but by February it's hard to find a lot of the people who joined in

January. Pubs want to know you are going to stay active long after your initial month. The good ones are looking for three months of consistency.

I can't say this strongly enough: Get your profile in order before you go knocking on a publication's door.

In case you've forgotten what we've talked about in chapter 5:
- Pick a username
- Add a picture
- Write a biography
- Connect your social accounts

HOW TO FIND PUBS AND SOLICIT TO WRITE WITH THEM

Searching for publications on Medium is tedious, but it's a good place to start. When you use the search key to add topics you are interested in writing about, a few pub suggestions come up. Click through those pubs and see what they're like. Most list what they are about and what kind of submissions they prefer, as well as a link to their application.

Treat a submission like a job interview. If you're a writer, this is your business. Treat it like a profession that earns money for fun things and pays the bills. Pubs have a lot of benefits, like followers and promotion capabilities. Those are great benefits, and you want them in your corner. Be kind and professional.

Make sure you are a good fit for the pubs before you send an application. If you want to write about writing, then don't apply to write with a fiction pub. Make sure you've read the about page and like to write suitable content.

If you want to know more about a particular publication, visit the pub page. Most have about pages and/or FAQs. Most go to great lengths to tell you what kind of content they publish and what's allowed or not allowed on pieces you may want to publish with them.

If a pub doesn't have published material like this, you can read the pieces it has published to make sure you write the kind of content they publish and can format your work in a desirable way to get it published.

Take the time to discover what a pub requires and accepts so that you know you are a good fit for the pubs you solicit. If you are a good fit, then submit an application.

Do you walk into a job interview before you know what the company is about? Probably not. Not if you want to get hired. Submitting an application is the same as applying for a job.

Send a draft/don't click publish

If you're a writer, here's another question you wrestle with:

Q: *Which goes first, the draft or the published piece?*

I get asked this question all the time. This one has an answer.

A: *The draft goes first.*

The first time I shared this answer people looked at me like I had three heads.

A lot of people asked me, "Are you sure"?

One person said, "Your perspective has changed since starting your pub."

Undoubtedly, my perspective has changed, so I studied the question thoroughly, and on this point my answer is unchanged.

Medium agrees. Quoting directly from Medium FAQs:

The workflow is simple. Writers submit drafts to editors, who have final say on what stories appear in a publication and their final form. Editors can write their own stories, and for collaboration can review, correct, leave notes, and approve stories by other writers according to the standards of the owners of the publication.

There's even a diagram.

If you are submitting a new story to a publication, it should follow these steps. The workflow is simple. Writers send drafts to pubs and when pubs publish, the piece appears on your profile.
It's the healthiest relationship possible between writers and pubs. It's how it's supposed to be. It's how to maintain a well-balanced writer diet.

I've never had a story refused to be published on the basis of it being a draft. I've had many refused on the basis of them being already published.

Don't hit publish. That's the pub's job.

If you publish first, your story won't show on the pub page because it will immediately fall to the original date it was published.

A publication might accept an already-published piece, although a strong tide is turning against this practice. Pieces that are already published do not perform as well as fresh or draft stories that the publication publishes and promotes.

WHY DOES A DRAFT MATTER TO SOME PUBS AND NOT OTHERS?

What is the publication's job? To publish great pieces, right?

Do you publish first?

Nope. Not unless you're self-publishing a book - and you're not doing that on Medium, unless you're spreading it out over multiple stories.

You send it to the publisher and let the publisher publish it.

While some publications may accept pieces published to your profile, this is not desirable.

Sending a piece with highlights and claps to a publisher is not good practice.

Do you remember taking algebra? To solve an equation we follow the order of operations: "Please Excuse My Dear Aunt Sally" or PEMDAS. Parenthesis, Exponents, Multiplication, and Division, from left to right. Then Addition and Subtraction, from left to right. Follow the order of operations; they're proven and they work. Plus, you get to the correct answer every time.

Be patient and follow the steps.

This is not the place to be trendy and try something different. This is the place to follow the rules. Send a draft to the publication every time, then wait for the publication to publish it.

If you are sending a piece that's already on your profile, here's what you're saying: "I've already published this piece. Just slap your label on it." There's nothing warm and fuzzy or healthy about this kind of relationship. The publication should be your first stop when publishing your piece, not your last stop.

When a writer bleeds on the page, he wants to share his emotions with the world quickly, but publishing first isn't the best way to accomplish this. Doing so circumvents the process and minimizes the pub's readership, connections, introductions and contacts.

Since you are sending your work to a pub, you know they have valuable connections and influence. Let the influence work for you in the best way possible.

The process is simple and proven. Submit a draft, then wait for the pub to publish the piece.

Don't shut down opportunities by publishing first. It's not the proper order of operations. It's not how it's supposed to be. The draft gets sent to the pub and when the pub publishes the story it will appear on your profile. If you're solving a math equation, you follow the order of operations. Do the same thing with your publications when sending new stories for publication.

HOW DO YOU NOT HIT PUBLISH?

It's easier than you think, but it isn't intuitive unless you are familiar with the process. After you've selected your tags and whether or not you want your piece to be locked, don't click publish now on the preview screen. Instead, close that window, drop down from the three dots, and add your piece to a publication and confirm.

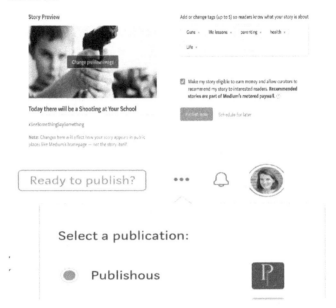

Don't make substantial edits after the pub has published a piece

Every piece sent to a publication should be as clean as possible and in final form.

That said, we all know that editors are human, too. If you catch a typo after a piece is published, edit it and move on.

Do not - I repeat: DO NOT make material changes after a piece has been published.

Let me put my parent hat on for a second.

I often tell my kids, "Just because you can doesn't mean you should."

All joking aside, just because you can edit a piece doesn't mean you should. Be cautious about clicking the gear to edit a piece after the pub has published it. The pub edits the piece into final form, and making changes after the piece has been published circumvents the process.

Think about guest posting. If you guest post on someone's blog, you can't make changes without going through the website owner. It's the same thing here. Don't make material changes after the pub has published a piece.

WHAT'S A MATERIAL CHANGE?

What's a material change? The answer to this question varies from pub to pub. If a pub doesn't accept locked stories - stories that earn money - locking a piece may be a material change. If a pub doesn't want tags changed, changing tags may be a material change. If you are adding substantial verbiage, you are making a material change. If in doubt, don't do it, or seek permission. It's not worth damaging your relationship with your pub or causing yourself to be removed as a writer. Many pubs say repeat offenders will be removed. You don't want to be one of them.

A gentle reminder: pubs can accept a limited number of writers. They can easily remove a squeaky wheel for a talented newcomer. Exercise care.

PULL PIECES WITH CARE

Everyone wants the best performance for their story, but not all stories are a home run. When a story doesn't perform well, you may consider pulling it back from a publication. Do this carefully.

On occasion, I have pulled a piece from a publication, but only with extreme care. I recommend you not pull a piece until you have carefully considered other options. Publications receive a notification when you pull, or remove, a piece. They can quickly see when you submitted the piece, how long it was in their queue and when
you pulled it.

In edit mode (click on the gear), from the

Share

Remove story from publication

Cancel editing

three dots, you have the option to remove a story from a publication.

If you are pulling a piece, do so before it is published, if at all possible, and make sure the piece is not scheduled before you pull it. If editors have spent time editing your piece and preparing it for publication, they aren't going to be happy receiving notice that you've pulled it after they've spent their valuable time on your story.

Publishous syndicates pieces across our website, which has a ridiculously high number monthly views. If we've prepared your piece for publication, syndicated it on the website and put extra promotion behind it, we're less than excited to see that it's been pulled because we've invested a bunch of time and effort in promoting your work.

If you've been offered a book contract and your contract dictates previously published forms cannot exist, we'll celebrate with you. Contact us and we'll work to together to pull your pieces. Communication is key.

If you are playing the stats, turnaround time, and regularly remove pieces, the publication reserves the right to remove you as a writer.

Pulling a high performing piece that the pub's connections and eyes helped make a success is not a good way to offer warm fuzzy feelings. If you've used the pub for success, you should exercise extreme care in pulling the piece.

BEST COMMUNICATION TIPS

Consider the publication you want to write for. Depending on when the pub opened, it can be serving up to 2,000 writers. Can you imagine the volume of those inboxes if each of those writers was to email the pub and how it may affect turnaround time of publishing pieces?

The time to get a piece published increases for every writer with stories in the pub queue. Everyone is best served when you streamline communication as much as possible.

As a new writer, you'll have common questions many others have already asked. Pubs who have answered common questions generally make answers available and easy to find on the publication homepage. You'll be surprised how many Medium questions can be answered in Google search.

- **Do** visit the pub homepage, About page, FAQ page for common Q & As, to find answers.
- **Do** a Google search for technical questions.

- **Do** ask questions of people in your writing groups.
- **Do** respect the pub's decision to not accept new writers for a period of time-- they are probably developing ways to serve you better.
- **Do** send a piece to the pub queue instead of asking the pub "Will you accept this story for publication?" (This assumes you've been accepted as a writer. If you are not already a writer, follow the application process, which is different for each pub).
- **Do** check your story often to see if it has been scheduled for publication instead of asking if/when a story will be published. **Note**: If your story hasn't been published in 5-7 business days, it's reasonable to assume it is not going to be published. Weekends and holidays are not business days and do not count.
- **Do** turn on notifications and check them often for status about whether a piece has been accepted, scheduled, published.
- **Do** check notes on a piece to see if there is something you need to do in order for your story to get published.
- **Do** streamline communication by using locked notes (more on that below).

Don't: Ask a question if you haven't sought out the answer using the methods above.

Don't submit more than 3 pieces at a time. This varies from pub to pub, but don't expect more than one piece to be published per day.

Most pubs want to be helpful. It's probably the reason they set up shop. If there's an issue only the pub can handle, then email the publication.

Seek out a few good pubs and foster a good relationship.

Hack the pub search by using Smedian: (https://toppubs.smedian.com/). You can request to write with multiple publications quickly.

Smedian updates its top publication rankings on a weekly basis.

Publishing with pubs is the best way to get eyes on your work before you have developed followers. Once you have a following, publishing with pubs continues to be the best way to share your work with different people who may not be among your followers.

Don't forget to tag your piece.

What are tags?

That's the topic up next.

Ch 7: What are Tags and How do I use them?

Adding tags is another way to increase the visibility of your writing. If you are a blogger think keywords. What keywords are to a blogger, tags are to Medium. Don't beat yourself up if you have no idea what this means. In blogging a keyword describes the contents on the page. Think back to school when your composition teacher drilled you for the main idea. Keywords sum up the main idea of the entire post or story. Keywords form part of the metadata data. Therefore, keywords are important for search engine optimization or SEO.

In short, keywords help your work get found across the internet. Tags help your work get discovered on Medium. All relevant tags help, but some help more than others. Don't misuse tags. Medium usually suggests at least one tag and it auto prefills in the tag section, but you can add up to five tags. You should use all five because adding relevant tags helps your story get discovered by more people and in more categories, especially if you use top performing tags.

Don't tag your work with tags that aren't relevant. If someone is searching for relevant topics, your story may appear in Google search listings. I wrote a piece that came up at the top of a Google search for "healthy publications" (https://medium.com/the-mission/how-to-have-a-healthy-relationship-with-your-medium-publication-ef450cfeaf9e) for many months.

Search engines are changing the way they respond to tags because people are misusing their keywords and using ones that perform better for higher site ranking. Use relevant tags. It's more difficult to misuse tags if you publish via publications because they change your tags for appropriateness and performance.

At Publishous we make an effort to fill out the tags for our writers. If a piece has 4 of 5 tags filled in and none of them pertain to our major, high performing categories, then we fill out the last tag appropriately.

This is an easy way to improve the performance of your story. Most pubs will not do this for you. This is part of your job as a writer. Fill out your tags, and if you're submitting through a pub, make sure you have one tag that is relevant to that pub.

If a piece has no tags or just one or two tags filled in I wonder:
1. Does the writer not care about his/her tags?

2. Does she/he not know how important tags are to the performance of a story?

To be clear, this is not the publication's job. This is the writer's responsibility. On days the pub queue is brimming over with new stories, we cannot tag for you. You are responsible for the performance of your piece. Write good content and tag it. Many pubs want you to add at least one tag relevant to broad topics the pub promotes.

Publishous is set up with our five broad categories to reflect top-performing tags across the platform: Christianity; Productivity; Stories and Life, which also encompasses Short Stories and Life Lessons; "A Better You", which encompasses health, wellness, and relationships; and Writing. We're purposely set up for the top performing tags to enhance the performance of your story.

Every piece should be tagged before publication. Here's a recap:
1. Tag every piece
2. Use all available tags
3. Tag appropriately

Don't change tags after the story is published. Pubs change tags, usually to enhance performance or to accent the piece as pertaining to its commonly published topics.

If you're a top writer in a certain category, then add a locked note on your story. *I'm a top writer in Life Lessons and appreciate this tag.* The pub can make editorial changes to your story in accordance with Medium guidelines. Most of them want to help you, especially if you make it easy on them.

Add a locked note on the piece instead of sending an email and unnecessarily filling inboxes. Pubs are busy. As a parent I tell my kids: if you want someone to do something for you, make it easy on them. If you need to communicate something to the pub about your story, add a locked note with your request.

To create a locked note, highlight a selection of text, then click the lock. Add a note in the box at the right. Only you, the writer, and the editors of the publication can see the note, provided the piece is with a publication. Otherwise, only the writer and the sender can see the locked note.

nt on a summer mission trip t

only did I visit multiple count

ent on a **summer mission** trip that
t only did I visit multiple countries
d understanding things is not the s

If you have information relevant to the story, the editor needs to know leave a locked note on the story itself. It's simple and all the information is on the piece it pertains to.

Publishous writers who communicate in this fashion find their reasonable requests honored, especially because they have communicated in a simple, clear fashion and have not unnecessarily clogged up my inbox.

Your pubs will be grateful if you consider their time and communicate in simple, effective, time-saving ways. Adding locked notes on the piece they pertain to saves everyone valuable time and helps to keep the pub queue turnaround time low.

Ch 8: How do I Make Money with the Medium Partner Program?

Pop the champagne!

Are you ready for the best part of this whole thing?

Let's talk about making some money.

For many of you, this is the moment you've been waiting for.

As with all good things, there's a catch. You've got to follow the rules. This is where we're going to talk about what those are and how to deal with them.

You can earn money by writing stories and putting them behind the metered paywall. By doing so you agree to all terms and conditions as stated in Medium's Terms of Service. Revisit Chapter 3 to review the legalese. And there's more legalese to add. You must obey the Partner Program guidelines, as well as any other guidelines. The guidelines are clear to say you can't participate in the program unless, or until, you understand and comply with the terms fully. Your acceptance of using these attributes on the platform serves as your binding agreement that you understand and will be held to the terms.

When you check the box to make your piece eligible to earn money, you agree that you understand the guidelines for locked posts. Not following the rules can get you removed from the program.

Medium may remove a post from behind the paywall at any time, usually because it does not meet the qualification standards of a locked post, and will make reasonable efforts to inform you if a specific post does not meet the standards or that your account has been removed from the program.

Let's be clear: Medium is on your side. It opened the paywall potential for writers to earn revenue. They want you to succeed, and they want it to be fair for everyone.

LOCKED POSTS

For each locked post you have the chance to earn revenue based on various performance factors, including but not limited to reader engagement. Medium pays the writer money from subscription fees, as determined by Medium. Medium sends payment for any revenue earned during a calendar month after the month has ended and reserves the right to adjust the factors at any time.

Here is how an unlocked post appears:

Looking at the published piece is a good way to double check whether or not your post is locked. When a locked piece is published, the message is different. The message on a locked piece looks like this:

Only you can see this message.

This story is eligible to earn money through the Partner Program. It may be shown as part of the metered paywall.

CAN A LOCKED POST BE INCLUDED IN A PUBLICATION?

Yes, according to Medium guidelines, but not all publications accept locked posts. Make sure you send locked posts to publications that accept them. A writer who locks a post through a publication receives the same amount of money regardless if the post is published through a publication or posted to your profile individually.

When preparing a story for a publication, you may select the box to make a story eligible to earn money and allow curators to recommend your story. You may also adjust these settings by dropping down from the three dots in edit mode and adjusting the distribution and unlisted settings. The writer and Medium can lock or unlock a piece. If you think you've locked a piece that does not appear as locked, check your settings. See whether or not your piece is in compliance with locked piece guidelines. Double check whether you opted in during the publishing flow and make appropriate adjustments, if necessary.

If you believe your piece should be eligible for payment and you have opted in by checking the curation box, you may need to contact Medium for resolution. Before contacting Medium, make sure you are in compliance with locked post guidelines.

What content is not allowed in a locked piece?:

- You may not sell advertising.
- The purpose of the story cannot be to drive traffic to an external website.
- If you receive compensation, goods, or services for writing the post you must say so.
- Do not ask for applause or include calls to action requesting donations or use embeds to capture user information, i.e. do not add subscription boxes to grow your list.

People are paying to read member pieces. It is an ad-free zone. If you want to do the above, your piece needs to be unlocked.

BECOME A MEMBER

If you are a writer who locks posts, I hope you are also a member. The cost to be a member is nominal, not much more than a good cup of coffee, unless you pay the member fee as a one-time payment. Then it's even lower. As a member you can receive revenue and the membership fee pays for that benefit. It's that simple.

Support Medium with its member fee to read an unlimited number of stories and to have the ability to earn money. Support your publications by sending them revenue, too. Because you are earning revenue, a small portion should go back to those making it possible for you to put money directly into your pocket every month.

Unless you are a member, you can only read a handful of locked stories each month. Many writers serious about being here are locking pieces as an extra source of income. Some of them are making a full-time income by writing here. If you are supporting writer friends and making a presence here, you should also consider membership. As a member your applause helps other writers earn money.

What other benefits do members receive?:
- Unlimited access to read ad-free stories
- Curated daily selections

- Monthly magazine

If that sounds like too many emails, you can adjust your email settings to your liking.

Adding a soft call-to-action with a link to an external list-building landing page is golden. This opportunity wasn't always available on member pieces, but this has changed. Heed caution: a soft CTA (call-to-action) is allowed. Member pieces are supposed to be ad-free. People are paying to read this content, not to have advertised goods and services pushed at them.

You also need to set-up your Stripe account.

SET UP STRIPE

Stripe is the way you get paid. Stripe is Medium's chosen method to pay you for your writing, but it is not available in all countries. Check to make sure your country is eligible to receive payment before setting up Stripe (https://stripe.com/global).

The bank account or debit card of your choice can be connected. Your full legal name, not a penn name, is required for set-up. Once you've added all of the legal information required by Stripe and finish creating your account, you're ready to make money.

One of the things you might not know is...

PUBS DO NOT RECEIVE REVENUE FROM LOCKED PIECES

Your monthly member fee goes to Medium, and Medium invests that portion back into its business by sharing it with writers who have engagement on their locked pieces.

A publication does not receive any revenue from the Partner Program based on having a locked post within the publication. The writer, not the pub, receives revenue from engagement on locked pieces.

This needs to be restated because writers are confused on this point.

The writer receives revenue from a locked post. The publication does not. The publication does not receive any revenue from a locked post.

From the time publications started, they have not been making money by being on the Medium platform. Publications, by and large, are providing these services for free, so many of them have moved to a sponsorship model.

What this means for you is that some pubs will make you pay to join. Others will give their paying members priority to have their pieces published before non-paying members and give their paying members extra benefits.

Said differently, your publications, unless stated clearly, do not earn revenue on Medium.
If you make money, share the love and consider supporting the publications you publish through.

If you're wondering why you're in the pub queue longer than others whose pieces seem to come up more quickly, ask yourself if you're supporting the pubs who are helping you earn income, then register your support.

Publishous has various writer membership options and support levels: Our writers can become members here: publishousnow.com/join-us/ . Supporters can become partners here: publishousnow.com/partner-with-us/. You can begin your support today. If you like the services we provide to writers, we appreciate your support.

Many writers write for years before they earn money from their craft. This is a glorious day. You're on your way to making money.

Celebrate!

What's that?

You're an overachiever and want even better performance for your stories? I like your spunk.

You may be in pursuit of the elusive curation.

Ch 9: How do stories get curated?

What is curation?

Curation is a boost provided by Medium to give your piece extra exposure. Specifically, Curators are a small group of people Medium has reviewing thousands of stories every day. If your piece is selected for curation, it means huge benefits. Your story gets shared by Medium via emails to subscribers who follow the topics you write about. Curated stories enjoy extra promotion and the more eyes that fall on your story, the more engagement it is likely to receive. If promotion is to writers what location is to realtors, we can all happy dance about promotion, promotion, promotion.

Curators add your story to relevant topics. Back to those tags and keywords. Use appropriate ones--it matters. Then your story gets distributed to people interested in those topics across Medium's homepage and through email. If you're opted in, and you should be opted in to a minimal level of notifications if you are serious about being successful on this platform, you've probably noticed the suggested reads across the bottom of your email. That's part of curation. While you won't see your own story under curation selections, you will see other curated selections, and others will see your story being curated.

HOW DOES CURATION HAPPEN?

There is no textbook answer.

The piece I think is going to flop will be curated, while the piece I'm positive will be curated gets passed over. It's mind-boggling.

It's because there's a human element to the selection process. That's both good and bad. Real-life people, not bots, are actually reading your words, the craft you've cried over, laughed about, stressed over, worked for hours on and bled sweat onto the keyboard so your words can come to life across a page. You want your words to be read but to be read by someone who can open additional promotion of your craft is an extra bonus.

The downside is there is no set strategy to get curated. There is no set of checkboxes to ensure curation. You might do everything right and be completely passed over by the curation team. It doesn't mean your work is bad; it just means that the people on the curation team didn't notice it this time. The team is a small group of people who have diverse interests and read thousands of stories every day.

This is why consistent publishing on the platform is so important. Publish often so the eyes meant to find your work will see it. People meant to see your words will read them if you keep showing up.

It's a beautiful thing, curation.

There's no set formula, but curators look for certain things.

These tips won't ensure curation, but they are a helpful, not exhaustive, list, as the human component is nothing any algorithm can capture.

QUALITY

Quality over quantity. Posts with a story-telling quality or ones that share something useful and in a creative way. Listicles are largely absent from curated pieces. A listicle is content presented in the form of a list. A lot of people chunk out content in list form. I've done it myself on occasion, but did not expect a listicle to garner curation. It's the kind of content to fall back on when you need to get something out quickly, are in a writing challenge, or are trying to meet a certain number of pieces published in a week.

Most listicles don't require a lot of thought. I created one for the fun of it. The title was "40 things you don't know about me, and I hope I don't bore you to death." It earned a fair amount of applause, but I knew it wouldn't get curated. It wasn't worthy of the promotion. Work that is well thought-out, in-depth effort gets curated.

The human component is once again accented and punctuated with humor by my finding a listicle that earned curation directly after writing this section. You just never know what will get curated, but it is a beautiful thing.

HEADLINES

Simple, straightforward headlines that accurately describe what the story is about tend to catch the curator's eye. Clickbait titles perform well for ratings, but curators tend not to select them. Profane titles and titles with all capitalization don't gain favor.

IMAGES

Every story needs a Creative Commons (CC) image. On Medium, you may use a video from YouTube, Vimeo, Twitch, Vine and similar sites, as long as the site gives permission for its use.

PROFILE

Your profile should be set-up well with a picture, name, and biography.

WELL-EDITED

Your piece should be well-edited and free of major typos and grammatical errors. Nothing will ever be perfect, but your writing should be as error free as possible. Don't over-edit. Do have a well-edited piece.

WRITE FROM THE HEART

Writers who are curated often write about topics they care deeply about so the emotion comes through in their writing. Sometimes they write from a personal experience or from a unique perspective on a subject. Don't think about curation while you are writing. Don't worry about performance measures. Just let the words flow. Reading the piece aloud for flow catches edits that cannot be made with the help of apps. Bonus points for making the reader get in touch with your writing in an emotional way. Write about what moves you in a way that moves others.

What else is helpful?

Keeping an eye on your stats.

What are stats and how do I read them?

That's up next.

Ch 10: How to Read Stats and Understand What They Mean

Are you the person who watches and analyzes everything about your stats or the person who watches them as little as possible? I don't watch my stats often, unless I'm deep in the trenches trying to learn something about how the platform works or how it has changed again. The one constant is change. The first thing to tip me off that something has changed is my weekly payout from the dashboard, which causes me to look at my stats to see if performance has changed. If it's higher than expected, I can guess some stories have been curated. If the payout is lower than expected, it causes me to look at the stats to see what is happening on my stories.

Have I missed the mark somewhere?
Did I not promote my work well enough?
Is something new or different happening on the platform?

A look at the stats is in order to see what is happening and if there are any simple solutions for improvement.

Visit your profile. Scroll down from your profile to stats.

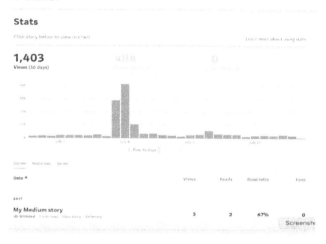

The graph shows your traffic over the last 30 days. I make mental notes of what story links I share in which writing groups and note the comparison with spikes in traffic. Patterned behavior means this takes no effort or time. I stay abreast of which share threads offer the best traffic and share links on them accordingly. Line up a newly released post with a strong share thread if possible.

Views and reads are slightly different. Views are the number of people who have clicked through to your story and read some of it, while reads represent the number of times people have read all the way to the bottom.

Fans are the number of people who have clapped for your story.

When you click on the story you receive specific information relevant to that story. All of these numbers are estimates. You see total views, lifetime earnings, and read ratio for your story. Lifetime earnings is the total revenue you have made for your story as of the previous week, if you've published through the partner program.

You also see the source of traffic for your views. This shows the average number of people who have clicked through links shared across social media platforms: Facebook, Twitter, LinkedIn and others.

Ch 11: How do I promote my work and other questions?:

Promotion is easy if you're in good writing groups. I'm in several writing groups where daily and weekly share threads are offered. A share thread is the opportunity for writers to add a link of your writing on a common share thread where other writers are doing the same thing. Everyone who shares a link also works the thread by engaging and sharing pieces written by other authors. All of my writing groups are on Facebook. These are groups where writers applaud, highlight, comment on, and promote each other's writing.

Connection and influence are equally important. Writers share their connections with each other. A healthy group will engage with your work and share it in their circle of influence. Writers are good at introducing connections to other writer friends for mutual benefit of one to another. It won't take you long to figure out who the generous members of the group are. They are those who share your work on other social platforms, applaud it, and comment to increase engagement.

You'll probably find that members of these groups come up with creative ways to market you and your work. The collective nature of one person's idea sparks an idea from someone else, and in a short time you have a bank of probable solutions.

Other writers are good at giving honest feedback on your writing, too. If a piece doesn't perform well, it's a good way to get feedback for growth. Ask questions like: Why do you think this didn't perform? What could have worked better?

Writing groups are an excellent source of collective resources. Ask a question and someone in the group usually has the answer or knows someone who has expertise. Most people are willing to be helpful and share their knowledge and abilities.

It's all based on trust. You don't give with the idea of getting something in return, but a common reciprocity is expected. Don't take more than you give. No one likes a taker. It's natural to give with other people who are doing the same thing. It's human nature to want to help those who have helped you.

These groups are places where connection and encouragement happen. General questions can be asked and answered. Support and feedback are offered. It's all about connection and a level of trust naturally develops. Here's what it looks like, specifically.

CONNECTION, INFLUENCE, AND BEING SOCIAL WITH WRITING GROUPS

You need to connect with a group of writers who you can support and encourage you. When you are weary, they will hold you up. If you have a good group of online writers, someone will be able to respond quickly, especially if you have global members. When someone is sleeping, someone else is awake. They will help you gauge your aptitude and capabilities. When you break or have a breakthrough, you can get help or celebrate with someone who will respond right away.

One way to connect with other writers is to go to Facebook and search for writing groups.

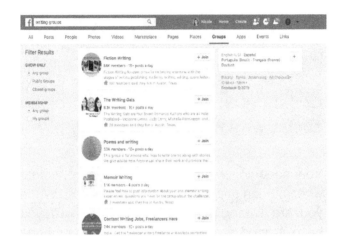

Find a handful of writing groups that are relevant to what you want to write about, have at least 500 or more members and show active posting because these groups are established and active. Most writing groups have daily or weekly share threads where everyone posts a link, soliciting others' engagement.

I encourage you to post your links and share others' links. When you share someone's link, be sure to tag them so they know who their most valuable supporters are. Add a hashtag or two for an even more valuable share.

Some writer groups allow a one-time "I'm new here" post. You only get one chance at this, so add as much information as you can and make it as valuable as possible:

- State this as your first or "I'm new post"

- Tell who you are and what you write about
- Share a newly published piece and ask for feedback
- State a goal as a call to action: "I'd like to have 100 new followers by the end of the day. Who are my new friends? I'll follow you back."

Not all groups allow a newbie post, so only do this if it's allowed. If it's not allowed, make an "I'm new here and want to connect" kind of post. If you are not sharing a link to your writing, most will allow you to:
- Introduce yourself
- Share what you write about
- Connect within the group or on a particular platform.

Follow up with people who respond and make new friends. Look for them on share threads and share their work and expand your reach by continually making new friends, sharing their work, and offering knowledge.

Be an active part of an active, healthy group with people you help and trust, and your work will receive an extra boost.

A lot of writers I know are introverts. They find themselves secluded and without connection. If these famous authors had social media they might not have been reclusive:

J.D. Salinger wrote *The Catcher in the Rye* as his first full length novel and some anthologies of shorter work followed later. When he died in 2010, he hadn't been interviewed in nearly 30 years.

Thomas Pynchon was awarded a National Book Award for *Gravity's Rainbow* in 1973 and sent someone else to accept it on his behalf. His person is shrouded in mystery and wild theories have developed as to his true identity, even that Pynchon may be a nome de plume for J.D. Salinger.

Harper Lee is the quintessential favorite for getting it right the first time. *To Kill a Mockingbird* is her only known book published to date. She's famous for declining interview requests. In 2007 she was asked to speak to the Alabama Academy of Honor. Her declination included this remark, "Well, it's better to be silent than be a fool." Don't we wish more people would adopt her approach on speaking, especially on social media?

Emily Dickinson was eccentric, to say the least. Some would call her just plain weird. She published about 1,800 poems in her lifetime. For the last two decades of her life she did not leave her family property and listened to her own father's funeral through a cracked door. Modern standards may call her one strange cookie.

Edgar Allen Poe's fictional monsters leapt off the page into his real life. The horror writer was plagued in life by his own demons of melancholy and paranoia. His poem *Alone* is credited with utterance of his personal torment and isolation.

J.K. Rowling is a rags-to-riches darling who has reached global fame. Rare is the writer who reaches such levels of fame while living. Her Harry Potter books are household names and she lives under a glaring spotlight but managed to publish *The Cuckoo's Calling* under a pen name before being found out.

Whether introverted or extroverted, writers and creatives tend to be weird and quirky. As much as we value seclusion to develop our craft, we need connection, too. It's no wonder we call our groups of like-minded people "support" groups. We need connection, and it seems that the people we let into our inner circle are selected with scrutiny.

In tribal times women would cook in a community kitchen. Today we eat in our homes, but tribes ate community meals. Men would hunt in groups. It's hard to say whether it took more manpower to bring home a kill big enough to feed a tribe, or whether it developed a sense of camaraderie, or both. It's the modern day friends with benefits and I don't mean hooking up or taking a roll in the hay. Trust is essential.

Wrap-up

There are a couple of questions I hear repeatedly:

Q: Should I publish to my blog or on Medium first?

I've heard this question answered both ways by seasoned people. You can do either, based on your goals and desired outcome.

As for me, I like to add my content to Medium first and use it as a testing ground. Whether on Medium, or on your blog, the content has a little fluidity, even after the initial time you click publish. When adding content to Medium first, you get feedback.

The kind of applause and comments you receive tells you something about how your audience will receive the piece. The engagement you receive on Medium tells you something about how your blog audience will receive the piece and, whether the engagement is positive or negative, there's a chance to revisit and revise it before presenting it again.

The people who have given me their email address, my subscribers, are my most coveted possession as a blogger. Like Hallmark, when you care enough, you send them the very best.

My first crack at a piece is seldom my best. After a little time passes I've thought of a way to say something better. I like to wait about a month between Medium and placing refined content on my blog, usually with a different headline and featured image and backlink to the original source, which is the place the piece was first published.

Medium seems to be somewhat insulated from this, but it is important to note that Google holds back its Google favor based on "sameness." If the piece is identical in different places on the web, it gets less favor in Google rankings. If the piece is different, perhaps a different keyword or even the same keyword with a different word count, it receives more Google love. Google is currently reevaluating its algorithms based on a human connection. We don't yet know the effect of the changes.

Conversely, some people are in favor of publishing to their blog first. They see their subscribers as valuable and give their first content to them. Subscribers get what no one else has read and receive the prized first read. About a week later, writers use the import tool to bring a piece over from the blog to Medium. It is important not to copy and paste, but use the import tool because a small piece of code appears at the bottom of your piece, "as

originally published on <u>the name of your blog</u>".
The backlink is automatically added for you.
The love Google will give is already connected
from one place to another across the web and
in place with the backlink.

But, and it's a big one, your piece needs to be
carefully proofread if you use the import tool.
The import tool is clunky and leaves out parts of
your original piece. I have yet to transfer a
piece from my blog to Medium that does not
require substantial copy and pasting of missing
content from the import process. I prefer not to
waste tIme In this way. Trust me, I can find
plenty of other ways to waste time, which is why
I don't want to do it here. I favor original content
on Medium and refine it for my blog audience.

Q: How do I balance how often to publish to my blog vs. publishing on Medium?

This question has a lot of variables. Ideally,
you're posting to each once a week. Some of
you just turned off and said "no way" while
others of you said "no problem". It depends on
how prolific a writer you are and how long it
takes you to write a post. Some big names
suggest publishing 4-5 times a week on
Medium alone while others say a couple of
quality pieces, upwards of 1200 words, will do
fine.

Practice, practice, practice. The more often you write the faster you become at developing desirable content quickly. Write often. Write daily. The more you practice, the lower your time commitment will be. If you are a writer who shows up occasionally to practice your craft, it takes a significant amount of time to write a piece of content worth publishing.

Big names say to publish daily, and I'm not as sure about this, especially if you know your content is not desirable. Writing challenges are good for developing consistency but not as good at helping writers develop quality content.

I'd rather publish a quality piece 2-3 times a week than publish crap. It may take 2 or 3 days of writing to get one piece worth publishing. Write daily, but publish quality.

You're ready.

You're Ready!

Since you've read through to the end and followed the instructions in each chapter, you have done everything it takes to present your best writer-self on Medium and create a growing following of staunch supporters.

You are poised for growth. You know what to do and how to do it well: how to set up your profile, how to earn followers, how to write meaningful stories with headlines that matter. You know how to support others and earn their respect and trust for promotion. You know how to engage with stories in a meaningful way. You have a pub's perspective from the inside-out and know how to treat pubs right and foster good relationships with them.

Are you inspired to act? I hope so.

You know what to do. It's time to do it!

Share your success stories.

If you've found helpful information won't you leave an honest review on Amazon?

As updates across the platform happen, I'll update them on my website. Get direct updates and follow me and the publication for the most up-to-date notifications.

References

Bezos, J. P. (2019, February 7). *No thank you, Mr. Pecker*. Retrieved from https://medium.com/@jeffreypbezos/no-thank-you-mr-pecker-146e3922310f

Carr, D. (2014, May 25). A platform and blogging tool, Medium charms writers. *The New York Times*. Retrieved from https://www.nytimes.com/2014/05/26/business/media/a-platform-and-blogging-tool-medium-charms-writers.html

Medium. (2018, May 25). *Privacy policy*. Retrieved from https://medium.com/policy/medium-privacy-policy-f03bf92035c9

Medium. (n.d.). *Help center: Your facts*. Retrieved from https://help.medium.com/hc/en-us/articles/215108608-Your-stats

Medium. (n.d.). *Medium FAQs and help center*. Retrieved from https://help.medium.com/hc/en-us/search?utf8=%E2%9C%93&query=medium+partner+program

Patel, N. (n.d.). How to create mobile friendly content [Web log post]. Retrieved from https://neilpatel.com/blog/how-to-create-mobile-friendly-content/

Sun, T. (n.d.). *How to set up a Medium account.* Retrieved from https://nealschaffer.com/how-to-set-up-a-medium-account/

Note: Affiliate links are included in this book, which means I receive compensation when you purchase products from these links.

About the Author

Nicole Akers has been a writer for as long as she can remember. At the tender age of 10, she wrote her first book, "The Day the Pencils Came to Life." The limited release first edition (i.e. the only handwritten) copy still holds a prominent position on her bookshelf.

As an adult, Nicole earned a BS in English, with minors in Creative Writing and Journalism from Indiana State University, where she graduated cum laude.
Nicole started her first blog in 2012 and joined Medium in early 2016.

In the Fall of 2017, Nicole set out to create a place where up-and-coming writers could get the exposure they both desired and deserved. In November 2017, Publishous was born. In less than 18 months, Nicole has built it to be one of the most popular publications on Medium, with over 12,000 subscribers. She has become a student of Medium.com and brings her hard-earned lessons to readers in her latest book, "Make Money on Medium."

CPSIA information can be obtained
at www.ICGtesting.com
Printed in the USA
LVHW110713280420
654653LV00003B/895

9 781072 566243